Copyright © 2021 Haughton'
All rights reserved

All rights reserved. No part of this workbook may be reproduced, distributed or transmitted in any form by any means, graphics, electronics, or mechanical, including photocopying, recording, taping, or by any information storage or retrieval system, without permission in writing from the publisher, Haughton's Love LLC, except in the case of reprints in the context of reviews, quotes, or references.

Haughton's Love LLC commissioned Stephanie Outten of Cocoon to Wings Publishing to create this workbook. The created content is proprietary with the exception of any cited work from outside resources. Users of this workbook are asked to act with integrity and not share content with anyone who is not a participant in the Just As I Am Coaching Program offered by Latarsha Haughton.

Printed in the United States of America

ISBN: 978-0-578-89731-8 (Paperback)

Published by Haughton's Love LLC
www.LatarshaHaughton.com

Scriptures marked KJV are taken from the KING JAMES VERSION (KJV): KING JAMES VERSION, public domain.

Scriptures marked NIV are taken from the NEW INTERNATIONAL VERSION (NIV): Scripture taken from THE HOLY BIBLE, NEW INTERNATIONAL VERSION® Copyright ©1973, 1978, 1984, 2011 by Biblica, Inc.™ Used by permission of Zondervan

Meet Your Self-Love Coach
Latarsha Haughton

Survivor | Overcomer | Thriver

Latarsha Haughton is an Inspirational Author, Transparent and Authentic Speaker, and Transformational Coach. She is the founder of Breaking the Silence... Healing the Pain and has endured decades of trauma – including sexual and emotional abuse. With the help of God, prayer, and trauma-informed therapy, after 30 years, she broke her silence. Today, Latarsha transforms that pain into purpose, and creates community for other survivors.

Her entrepreneurial experience includes her transformational life coaching practice: guiding men and women as they release wounds and embrace their power, and CEO of an assisted living community in Baltimore, Maryland, We Care First Assisted Living, LLC.

Latarsha sits on the board of directors at Women and Warriors on Route to Higher Heights Ministries (W.O.R.T.H.H.) and Journey to Joy Ministries, where she once received training in prayer ministry and abuse recovery. She holds an award for "Choosing to Live" from The Standing Still Alliance, an organization focused on domestic violence advocacy and awareness. Latarsha remains committed to studying biblical principles and rooting her ministries in the compassionate love of Christ.

Just As I Am: 12 Steps to Self-Love Coaching Program

"If you're searching for that one person that will change your life, look in the mirror." ~ Anonymous

When I think of my own personal journey, I am often flabbergasted that I can now look at myself and say, "I love Me!" I no longer have to wait for validation from someone else in order to feel love surrounding me. All I have to do is look in the mirror and see love looking back at me.

That wasn't always the case for me. I'm sure you can understand that by reading about my personal journey. That is why I have made it my mission to walk you through the 12 Steps to Self-Love that I had to go through in order to get to this place of healing and wholeness. It wasn't easy for me, and I know it won't be easy for you either. What I will promise you is that I am with you as you take each step because I've already carved the path for you.

Will you trust me to lead you on this journey where the final destination leads you to a place of wholeheartedly loving yourself, without conditions, flaws and all, and without the need for anyone else's validation? The mere fact that you signed up for this program tells me you are ready, even if you do not fully feel like you are there yet.

Over the next 12 weeks, I'll be walking you through loving you - Mind, Body, and Soul. We will address topics like:

MIND
- Knowing Your Identity
- Changing Your Mindset
- Boundaries and Distractions
- Letting Go and Leaving the Past Behind
- Reclaiming Your Power

BODY
- Flaws and All
- Treasuring Your Temple
- Uncovering the Hidden Gem

SOUL
- Soul Cleansing
- Forgiveness
- The Power of Connections
- Gratefulness

Our 12 weeks together will be broken down into the above three modules with a series of exercises in each module. We will spend five weeks in Mind, three weeks in Body, and the final four weeks in Soul.

Also, as a part of this program, I will be gifting you with two eBooks that truly blessed me as I began to walk out this process of loving myself. **Safe People: How to Find Relationships That Are Good For You and Avoid Those That Aren't** and **Boundaries: When to Say Yes, When to Say No, to Take Control of Your Life** by Dr. Henry Cloud and Dr. John Townsend. My prayer is you will read these books and apply the principles learned so that you can create the safe space within yourself that is needed for self-love to prevail.

Will you trust the process with me over these next 12 weeks? I hope you will. Let's do this together!

Latarsha Haughton
Your Self-Love Coach

MODULE ONE

MIND

MIND

Our mind holds the key to reclaiming our power. Did you know that? It took me years to learn that all of the horrible things that were done to me and said to me were planted like seeds in my mind. All it would take was for someone to water the seed - say one more negative thing, touch me the wrong way, yell my name like my father used to - and I was down on myself all over again.

I did not know then that I had the power to change my thinking in order to begin loving myself. Mahatma Gandhi said, "I will not let anyone walk through my mind with their dirty feet." That quote is pivotal to creating a whole new way of thinking, which is what you have to develop in order to love yourself so much that you don't need anyone else's validation to fill you up.

When I began transforming my mind by going to therapy for eight years, reading books about setting boundaries, healing from past trauma, and changing my circle, I found a love for myself that I never thought possible. It also opened me up to love God, my husband, and others more than I ever could when I was full of self-hate.

Through a series of carefully created exercises, you will discover how to stop playing "mental gymnastics" as Joyce Meyer calls it, and surrender your mind to only those thoughts that are healthy and good for you.

MIND
- Knowing Your Identity
- Changing Your Mindset
- Boundaries and Distractions
- Letting Go and Leaving the Past Behind
- Reclaiming Your Power

Let's Do This!

Mind
Knowing Your Identity

When you love yourself, it's so much easier for others to love you in return. Am I right? Believe me when I tell you I was full of lack of self-worth, not valuing myself or what I brought to the table in life and business. I simply hadn't learned to love myself because I didn't know myself - my true identity.

When you love yourself, you are open to giving yourself what you need and also receiving those things that make you feel good-good in your mind, body, and spirit.

8 Reason Why it is So Important to Love Yourself:
1. Because God loves you just how you are
2. When you love who you are, you accept who you are
3. It gives you confidence and approval
4. You stop being ashamed of yourself for everything you've done
5. When you love yourself, you look better
6. If you love yourself, others can better love you
7. You see more of the good about life than the bad
8. When you love yourself, the world around you changes

Exercise: I LOVE Me
In this exercise, you will write down 12 things you LOVE about yourself. These 12 things will help you know more about your true identity. Your list can be a combination of internal and external attributes. But, if you focus on the external, then include an explanation around why you love "that" about yourself.
After writing your list, stand in the mirror and read your list aloud. Smiling while reading your list enhances the experience. I've tried it for myself. Smiling allows you to be open to the experience of LOVE seeping into every crevice of your being.

I LOVE Me

"You are free, you are powerful, you are good, you are love, you have value, you have a purpose. All is well.." - Abraham Hicks

Use I AM statements to express why you love yourself. Ex. I LOVE Me because I AM a child of the King.

I LOVE Me because:
_____

I LOVE Me because:
_____

I LOVE Me because:
_____

I LOVE Me because:
_____

I LOVE Me because:
_____

I LOVE Me because:
_____

I LOVE Me because:
_____

I LOVE Me because:
_____

I LOVE Me because:
_____

I LOVE Me because:

_____

I LOVE Me because:

_____

I LOVE Me because:

_____

Song to Meditate On: *"Love Myself" by Hailee Steinfeld*

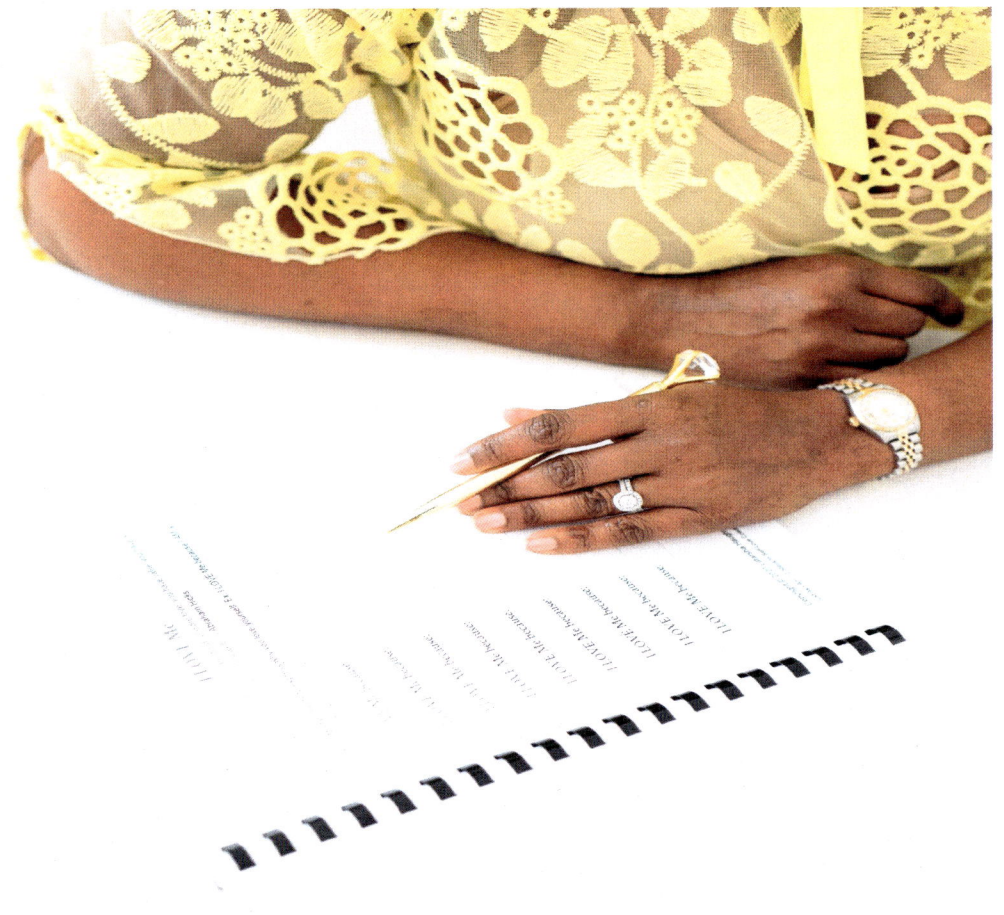

Mind

Changing Your Mindset

The mind is a battlefield. There is always a silent enemy trying to trick us and trap us into believing things about ourselves that are not true. The "silent critic" is lurking trying to steal our joy, kill our spirit, and destroy everything God made us to be.

Many of us who have been abused in some way. The silent critic is that voice we hear when we've experienced trauma that came to break us. The silent critic comes when our self-esteem has taken a blow. The silent critic is our own internal voice that was silenced when whatever happened to us happened.

How do you silence the inner critic? You must first change your mindset by:

- Identifying the lies
- Examining where they are coming from (what is triggering them?)
- Responding to the lies with the truth
- Beginning the healing process

Reflect on this scripture before moving into the exercise:
"I praise you because I am fearfully and wonderfully made; your works are wonderful, I know that full well. My frame was not hidden from you when I was made in the secret place, when I was woven together in the depths of the earth. Your eyes saw my unformed body; all the days ordained for me were written in your book before one of them came to be" Psalms 139: 14-16 (NIV).

Exercise: Silence the Inner Critic

In this exercise, you will begin to identify the lies you've been replaying in your head. You can't heal it if you don't identify it. This is your opportunity to stop the chatter and silence your inner critic that keeps telling you that you are not enough, you are not worthy, you are not loved. If you are a child of God, then you should know that you are all of these things and more.

Silence the Inner Critic

"Your inner critic is simply a part of you that needs more self-love."
— Amy Leigh Mercree

IDENTIFY THE LIES

List the top 5 to 6 lies you hear playing in your mind repeatedly:

EXAMINE WHERE THE LIES ARE COMING FROM (TRIGGERS)

Write the lie from your table above, and examine where that lie came from. What is triggering it? **As an example**, a lie that ran through my head was, *"You are stupid."* Everytime I messed up, I would hear that voice in my head telling me I was stupid. After going through therapy and sitting still with the Lord, I realized messing up or making mistakes was a trigger, and the voice telling me I was stupid was actually my father's voice I was hearing. He always told me I was "so stupid" any time I didn't do something the way he thought it should be done.

What are the lies you need to examine?

Lie #1

_____

Where did the lie stem from?

_____

What triggers the lie to come up for you?

_____

Lie #2

_____

Where did the lie stem from?

_____

What triggers the lie to come up for you?

_____

Lie #3

_____

Where did the lie stem from?

_____

What triggers the lie to come up for you?

_____

Lie #4

_____

Where did the lie stem from?

_____

What triggers the lie to come up for you?

_____

Lie #5

_____

Where did the lie stem from?

_____

What triggers the lie to come up for you?

_____

Lie #6

_____

Where did the lie stem from?

_____

What triggers the lie to come up for you?

_____

RESPOND TO THE LIES WITH THE TRUTH

For me, I had to go to the Word of God to help me replace the lies with the truth. Here are a couple of the scriptures I had to meditate on to break the lies from my psyche and replace them with the truth of what God said about me.

Lie: You are so stupid!

Truth: Proverbs 2: 6, "For the Lord gives wisdom; from his mouth come knowledge and understanding.

Lie: You are powerless!
Truth: Philippians 4:13, "I can do all things through Christ who strengthens me."

Maybe you do not yet know how to use scripture to replace the lies with the truth. That's okay! I didn't always know how to either, so I would pray and ask God to reveal His word to me. Google is very popular. You can search for scriptures related to the very thing you are being challenged with. Seek God's word for the truth, because the truth of who He says you are will set you free.

If you don't find a scripture to replace the lie with, then create a positive statement that will debunk what the lie tries to make you believe. As an example, using the "You are so stupid" lie, you can replace it with the truth, "I AM smart and wise. I know everything I need to know for when I need to know it."

Okay, it's your turn!

Lie #1

_____

Truth #1

_____

Lie #2

_____

Truth #2

_____

Lie #3

_____

Truth #3

_____

Lie #4

_____

Truth #4

_____

Lie #5

_____

Truth #5

_____

Lie #6

_____

Truth #6

BEGIN THE HEALING PROCESS

Healing is not something that comes overnight. It is not a quick fix solution to a problem. Healing takes time. It takes patience. Healing takes compassion, and it requires self-love.

Here are some things to consider to heal the inner critic in your mind:

1. **Attend therapy** - my abuse and trauma were so substantial, that I was left emotionally scarred. I had no idea how to love myself. I had to attend therapy for 8 years to get to a place of being healed, whole, and complete.
2. **Read books** - the saying, "reading is fundamental" is so true. Reading books was a fundamental part of my healing process. I will be recommending some books to you throughout the workbook.
3. **Share with your closest friend** - find someone who won't judge or criticize you for being critical of yourself.
4. **Allow yourself to feel the emotion of the criticism** - whenever you hear your inner critic, sit and listen to what it is saying. Allow yourself to feel where the emotion is in your body (your chest, your neck, your arms, etc.). Place your hand on that body part and tell it, **"I forgive myself for believing the lie. I will replace the lie with the truth, and I will trust the truth."**

In the chart below, write one-word steps you will take to heal your inner critic. Remember, this is not a quick fix, so list things that you will do over time. Set a schedule, if you need to, in order to stay on target with your healing plan.

Example of a Physical Step: **Walking**

Spiritual Steps	Mental/Emotional Steps

Physical Steps	Lifestyle Steps	Communication Steps

In the circle below, write in additional steps you will take. The circle represents the continuous work you will do to heal.

MY CIRCLE OF HEALING

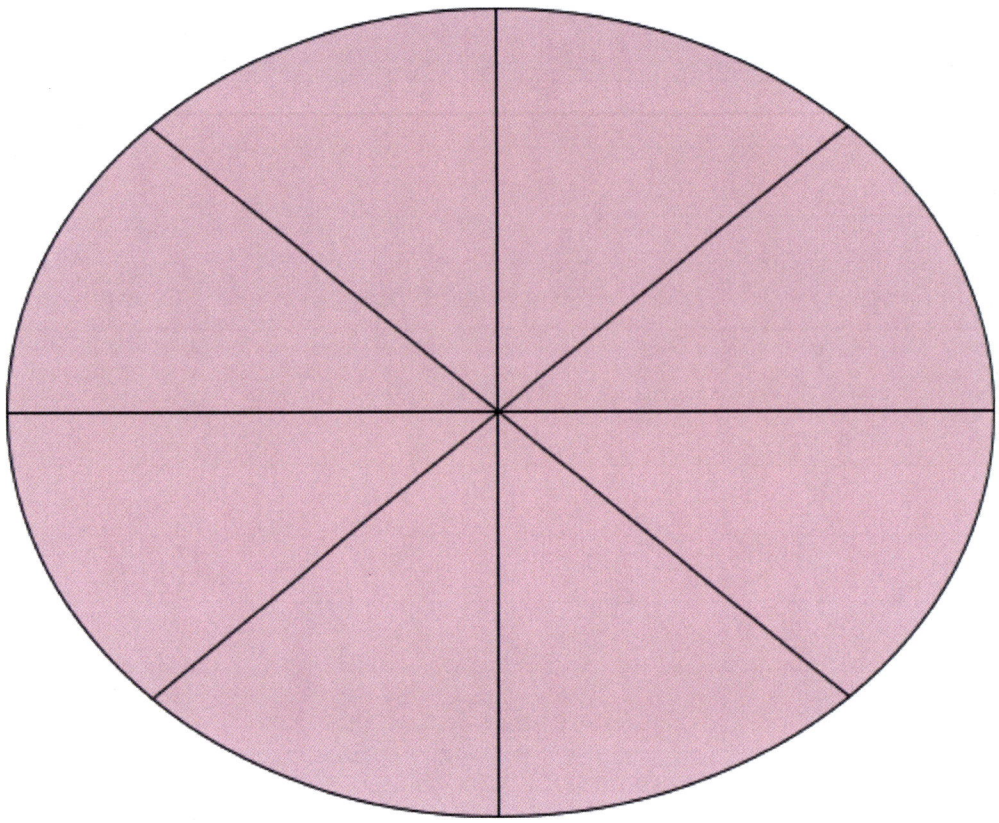

Song to Meditate On: "I Am Light" by India.Arie

Mind

Boundaries and Distractions

After experiencing trauma, it can be difficult to set boundaries in many areas of our lives. I was a "Yes" girl. I could not find the courage to tell people No. In my heart, I wanted to. But, my mouth would always betray me and cause me to say yes to things I wanted no part of.

According to the article, [What Are Personal Boundaries? How Do I Get Some?](#) the author shares six types of boundaries that people should set after experiencing trauma:

1. Material
2. Physical
3. Mental
4. Emotional
5. Sexual
6. Spiritual

[Exercise: What Are My Boundaries?](#)
In this exercise, you will identify the boundaries you should set in each of the 6 categories above. You will be given a process for communicating your boundaries so that you can effectuate the change you want to see in your life. When you love yourself, you set boundaries so that others cannot take advantage of you.

What Are My Boundaries?

"Lack of boundaries invites lack of respect.." - Anonymous

*Boundaries Defined:

- **Material boundaries** determine whether you give or lend things, such as your money, car, clothes, books, food, or toothbrush.
- **Physical boundaries** pertain to your personal space, privacy, and body. Do you give a handshake or a hug – to whom and when? How do you feel about loud music, nudity, and locked doors?
- **Mental boundaries** apply to your thoughts, values, and opinions. Are you easily suggestible? Do you know what you believe, and can you hold onto your opinions? Can you listen with an open mind to someone else's opinion without becoming rigid? If you become highly emotional, argumentative, or defensive, you may have weak emotional boundaries.
- **Emotional boundaries** keep you focused on your emotions while not feeling responsible for the emotions of others. Healthy emotional boundaries prevent you from giving advice, blaming or accepting blame. They protect you from feeling guilty for someone else's negative feelings or problems and taking others' comments personally. Being highly reactive in a situation suggests that you have weak emotional boundaries. Healthy emotional boundaries require clear internal boundaries – knowing your feelings and your responsibilities to yourself and others.
- **Sexual boundaries** protect your comfort level with sexual touch and activity – what, where, when, and with whom.
- **Spiritual boundaries** relate to your beliefs and experiences in connection with God or a higher power.

*Source: [What Are Personal Boundaries? How Do I Get Some?](#)

How to determine the boundaries you need to set:
1. Learn what's triggering you when asked to do something
2. Determine why it's bothering you (what's at the root of it?)
3. Feel where you're annoyed in your body (where are you tense?)

4. Figure out when you are most bothered by people's asks of you
5. Watch who you become when asked to do something you don't want to do

Answer this question:
What makes you think you are not worthy to set boundaries? _____

_____

_____

_____

Run to the closest mirror and tell yourself: **I AM WORTHY TO SET BOUNDARIES!**

Set Your Boundaries

Now that you know what types of boundaries there are, set one boundary in each of the boundary areas described:

Boundary Area	My Boundary
Material	
Physical	
Mental	
Emotional	
Sexual	
Spiritual	

Use these lines if you need more space to write out your boundaries in any of these areas:

_____

_____

Distractions

"Starve your distractions, Feed your focus." - Anonymous

dis·trac·tion

/dəˈstrakSH(ə)n/

noun

plural noun: **distractions**

1. a thing that prevents someone from giving full attention to something else.
"the company found passenger travel a **distraction from** the main business of moving freight"

2. extreme agitation of the mind or emotions.
"he knew she was nervous by her uncharacteristic air of distraction"

Source: Oxford Languages and Google - English

Distractions will come to rob you of your goals. Distractions are truly tricks of the enemy designed to throw you off focus and keep you from doing the things God has purposed for you to accomplish.

In my own life, I allowed people to be a huge distraction for me. For some of you, it might be people, too, or it could be social media, television, music, or a specific place. Whatever it is, it's time to let go of the distractions so you are fully available to fulfill your calling on this earth.

Before we go into the exercise, I wanted to share this YouVersion Bible app devotional I once read called, Right People, Right Place, Right Plan:

"In the story of Jonah, God sends Jonah on a mission to Ninevah, but Jonah disobeys. Instead, he heads in the opposite direction to Joppa, where he boards a ship to Tarshish. During the journey, a storm comes and the ship is in danger.

Have you ever stopped to think about the other people on the boat who were about to lose their lives besides Jonah? In fact, they were in danger *because* of Jonah. You see, sometimes all it takes is one rebellious, disobedient person to take down a whole shipload of people.

There are times in life when you are not the problem; the problem may be the people that you're associating with.

The boat to Tarshish was taking on water. Everyone was frightened for their lives, but it wasn't their fault. The problem was that they were associating with the wrong person—Jonah. Sometimes as soon as you get the wrong people out of your boat, your storm will cease.

Before the sailors threw Jonah off the boat, they tried rowing harder to bring the ship to land. But finally someone on the boat called a meeting and decided Jonah had to go. I'm sure they felt badly about it, but they knew that if they didn't throw him off, they were not going to make it to the other side.

Remember that when the sailors threw Jonah off the boat, God did not abandon him. He had already prepared a great fish to swallow him and spit him back onto shore so he could travel on to Ninevah, his intended destination. When you allow the wrong people to remain in your life, you are not helping them, but may be keeping them from what God has prepared for them.

Are there people in your life who are dragging you down? Ask God to reveal to you the people who need to be cut from your life and for wisdom in removing yourself from those relationships."

Exercise: What/Who Drains Me?

In this exercise, you will identify the people, places, things that have been draining your Yes's and stifling your No's. These are the things that have to go in order for you to reach your highest potential. These things will distract you from your destiny and keep you stuck. As you complete this exercise, notice if you see any trends in the types of people, places, or things that are draining you.

What/Who Drains Me?

"People inspire you, or they drain you. Pick them wisely." - Hans F. Hansen

I got to a point in my life where I recognized that someone I had been friends with for years, someone I shared a deep bond with (or so I thought) was sucking the life out of me. Ladies and gentlemen, raise your hands if you've ever realized someone in your life was an emotional leech?

It's not just people, though. Places and things can drain you as well. If I go back to my hometown, there are some places that remind me of my abuse and abusers. Pajamas actually were a thing that drained me. The very thought of wearing pajamas would send me into a panic. One of my abusers had easy access to me when I wore pajamas, so I would go to sleep fully clothed so it would either take him longer to get to me or stop him all together because it would take too long. He didn't want anyone finding out, so he needed quick access. I was not trying to give it to him.

Think about those emotional, physical, and spiritual leeches and list them below. I want you to list one person, one place, and one thing and how they drain you. **For example:** My abuser was the leech and he drained me emotionally, physically and spiritually. I wondered when I would ever be free of the abuse.

Remember to list one person, one place, and one thing:

1. _____
   _____

2. _____
   _____

3. _____
   _____

Exercise: Distraction-Free Zone

In this exercise, you are to create a distraction-free zone. This will be your safe space where no one and nothing can take you off focus. You will also want to ensure you designate an accountability partner to help you stay on track and away from the distractions.

Distraction-Free Zone

"Release the distractions that are holding you back and focus on one thing only: Getting it Done." - Anonymous

Our minds will take us to places we don't need to go simply so that we can get off of the path of productivity. Self-love is work. If you are constantly distracted by things that are not promoting love for YOU, then how will you ever fully know what it feels like to love yourself?

Creating a distraction-free zone is important because by doing so, you are giving yourself permission to focus on you.

Ways to create a distraction-free zone:

1. Create a schedule and stick to it. Block out time on your calendar when you will not be interrupted by anyone or anything.
2. Put your phone on Do Not Disturb during your scheduled distraction-free time.
3. Find a quiet space in your home or somewhere you feel safe to be, and stay there during your scheduled time.

In the boxes below, write out all of the ways you will create your distraction-free zone.

Song to Meditate On: "Jesus at the Center" by Israel Houghton and New Breed

Mind

Letting Go and Leaving the Past Behind

The real test of being able to free your mind after any form of trauma is when you can talk about the trauma without tears or constant flashbacks of the traumatic experiences. Whew! It took me a long time to get there, but I thank God I am finally free.

What will it take for you to fully let go and leave the past behind? How many more nights will you cry and feel guilty about what happened to you? Hear me clearly, your abuse had NOTHING to do with you! When people abuse others, whether physically, verbally, emotionally or otherwise, they have often experienced a form of abuse themselves and did not deal with it. So, it carried them into their future and caused them to inflict the same type of pain on others.

No more will I allow you to sit in that pain of your past. It is time to let go and leave the past behind. God has something so much greater for you. Let's discover what it could be!

Exercise: I Release and Let Go

It's time to let it all go! That's just what you will do in this next exercise. We get to choose what we will or will not hold onto. Will you continue to hold on to fear, doubt, unbelief, pain and negativity that you picked up because of your trauma? I hope your answer is NO.

With that said, let's release and let go...

I Release and Let Go

"Let go of the past, but keep the lessons it taught you." - Chiara Gizzi

When we've held onto our emotions for so long, it can sometimes be harder letting go that holding on. Have you ever noticed that when you let go of something that's been with you for a long time, you can sense that something is missing? This exercise will seem simple, but the magnitude of it will change the trajectory of your life.

Someone shared this exercise with me, and I believe it will benefit you greatly.

- Place a small object in your hand. It can be a coin, a pen, a piece of paper, etc.
- Hold your hand in front of you and hold on to the object tight for at least two minutes. Set your timer and pretend you are holding one of the limiting beliefs you've carried with you since your trauma occurred and your hand is the place inside of you where you hold onto paid (your gut, your psyche, etc).
- When time is up, open your hand and roll the object around in your hand for a few seconds.
- At this point, you are the one holding it in your hand, right?
- Okay, let it go!

How difficult was it for you to do that exercise? Circle one:

Not Difficult   Somewhat Difficult   Difficult   Very Difficult

Now, correlate this to the emotions you've been carrying around due to your trauma. How easy would it be for you to acknowledge that they are there, think about how they've held you in bondage, and then just let them go?

What would hold you back from doing that?

_____
_____
_____

List three (3) people that could hold you accountable to releasing and letting go of your painful emotions.

1. _____

2. _____

3. _____

Share why these three people are the right ones to hold you accountable on your journey to self-love.

1. _____

2. _____

3. _____

Answer this question: **ARE YOU READY TO RELEASE AND LET GO?**

Write your answer below. If you answer NO, schedule a 1:1 with me so we can discuss.

_____

Song to Meditate On: "Let Go" by Dewayne Woods

Mind

Reclaiming Your Power

The final section we will cover in the Mind will be all about reclaiming the power you lost when you experienced your trauma. It will take you doing some uncomfortable things, but I can tell you from my own experience that it will be so worth it.

What does it mean to reclaim your power? For me, it meant that I had to go back to the place where I lost it. It meant I had to relive some brutal moments. For you, it may mean coming face to face with the ones who hurt you. For others, it can be as simple as repeating a mantra to themselves over and over until they begin to believe it and it manifests in their life. God's healing plan is different for all of us, so be open to how He wants to heal you in this process.

Exercise: Do the Uncomfortable

Becoming free means you have to do some things that will hurt. You have to cry a little to have so much joy. Psalm 30:5 in the New International Version of the Holy Bible says, "...weeping may stay for the night, but rejoicing comes in the morning." That's one of my favorite scriptures to rest on. I hope you, too, can find comfort in it.

Grab some tissue. Men, please don't be afraid to let the tears flow. Our men hold so much in believing that if they break, everything around them will too. That's not true! It's in your tears that you will find sweet relief.

Find a quiet place where you will be free to do whatever it takes to reclaim your power. Take a breath, and let's begin...

Do the Uncomfortable

"I can do all things through Christ which strengtheneth me." - Philippians 4:13

I want you to think back to the day you lost your power. In a short story, write down everything you can remember. Here are some questions to ask yourself before you write it down:

1. Who was there?
2. What was I wearing? Be as specific as you can.
3. Where was I?
4. What happened?
5. When was the exact moment I knew my power was gone?

Share your story below. I want you to start the story with, **"I remember it like it was yesterday.."**

_____
_____
_____
_____
_____
_____
_____
_____
_____
_____
_____

_____
_____
_____
_____
_____
_____
_____
_____
_____
_____
_____
_____

Feel free to write on an additional sheet of paper, your notebook or journal if you need more space to write.

WHAT'S NEXT?

Now, here comes the hard part. Go in front of the mirror and read what you wrote aloud, but only loud enough for you to hear it if you are not alone in your home. I know it feels uncomfortable, but that's the point of the exercise, right?

In the callout cloud below, write the one word you felt when you read the experience out loud:

Whether you wrote a negative word or emotion or something positive like "FREE" in the callout cloud, I want you to write something positive about yourself in the callout star below. When I first shared my story, I still felt angry. But, I began to replace the anger with JOY because it was what I wanted to feel instead of the anger.

Once you have your word above, spend the day meditating on that word. I'd like you to do the following:

1. Write a sentence about yourself using the word in your callout star.
2. Repeat the word to yourself throughout the day.
3. Find a quote of Bible scripture that reflects the word, and write it on a post-in note that you will put up somewhere in your bedroom where you can see it.

Exercise: Reclaim My Power

You wrote out your pain story, and now it's time to write your power story. I shared with you earlier that I hate to wear pajamas because my abuser had easy access to molest me when I was in pajamas. As a full grown adult, I was still sleeping in my clothes. It wasn't until I got free

from the trauma and removed the stain of what the pajamas once represented, that I was finally able to start wearing pajamas. Now, I am a pajama junkie. I can't buy enough pajamas. With that one simple act of buying my first pair of pajamas and actually wearing them, I was able to reclaim my power.

How will you reclaim yours? Go back to your pain story and review what you wrote about the moment you lost your power. What can you take from that story to help you write your POWER STORY?

Write your story as if you are writing a letter to yourself.

My POWER Story

Dear _____, I am finally on the other side of my pain. Let me tell you what I did to get here so that you will always know what it means to be loved...

_____

_____

_____

_____

_____

_____

Song to Meditate On: "I See a Victory" by Kim Burrell and Pharrell Williams

MODULE TWO

BODY

Body

Flaws and All

Once the mind has done its work to hold us hostage to our past, then our body begins to feel the weight of the pain trapped in our mind. This is why it is critical that we change our mindset and learn who we are so we can bring a level of self-love to our body like never before.

Did you know that the body can heal itself? Louise Hay, motivational author and founder of Hay House, said, "My body is very wise; it knows how to heal itself." That is how awesome this temple is that God created.

1 Corinthians 3:16-17 says, "Don't you know that you yourselves are God's temple and that God's Spirit dwells in your midst? If anyone destroys God's temple, God will destroy that person; for God's temple is sacred, and you together are that temple." Wow, how powerful is that? I had to really sit back and read that scripture a few times, especially as someone who has been physically violated. God's word is clear; He will destroy anyone who violates His children's temples (bodies). So, if you are a child of God, you don't have to worry about getting revenge on your abuser. God's already got it under control

Okay, back to the body. When we've been abused, we tend to deal with self-esteem issues, low self-worth, or it can be the complete opposite where we become aggressive, conceited, and even promiscuous. We become these things in an attempt to mask who we are, or who we were when our innocence was snatched from us. Let's explore some of the ways we can win back the love of our body.

BODY
- Flaws and All
- Treasuring Your Temple
- Uncovering the Hidden Gem

Exercise: I'm - Perfect

Don't we all wish we had the perfect face, the perfect body, the perfect hair? The media shows us image after image of what is perceived as perfection, and we believe them. I had to learn for myself that I was made perfect in God's image. So, no matter what, I am perfectly imperfect.

In this exercise, you will lay down your mask and unveil the real you.

I'm -Perfect

"I saw that you were perfect, and so I loved you. Then I saw that you were not perfect, and I loved you even more." - Angelita Lim

im·per·fect

/imˈpərfəkt/

adjective

1. not perfect; faulty or incomplete.
   "an imperfect grasp of English"

Some of the synonyms found for this word are :

1. faulty
2. flawed
3. defective
4. shoddy

Source: Oxford Languages and Google - English

We often look at the word "imperfect" as one word. But, I like to look at it as two separate words, **"I'm Perfect."** If we look at it this way, it takes on a whole new meaning, right?

For this exercise, do the following:

Male Participants	Female Participants
<ul><li>Find your worst picture, the picture of yourself that you least like (it doesn't matter what age you were in the picture)</li><li>Print the picture in color</li><li>At the top of the picture, write in a black marker – I'm Perfect</li><li>Tape the picture to your refrigerator</li><li>Look at the picture everytime you go to the fridge and say aloud, "I'm Perfect!"</li></ul>	<ul><li>Take a picture of yourself bare-faced (no makeup and freshly washed)</li><li>If you are able to print the picture in color, do that</li><li>At the top of the picture, write in a black marker – I'm Perfect</li><li>Tape the picture to your refrigerator</li><li>Look at the picture everytime you go to the fridge and say aloud, "I'm Perfect!"</li></ul>

Exercise 2: I'm Flawed

We all have flaws. Own them. We were uniquely made, and even if we had a twin they would not look EXACTLY like us. There would be something different about them, something identifiable. That's how I like to look at flaws.

As a woman, I'm always held to a higher standard of beauty than a man would be. But men are held to a higher level of bravado and braun than a woman. What happens when we feel we don't live up to the beauty or the braun? We begin to see our flaws, which takes us from a place of self-love to self-loathing. Let's turn those flaws into our flawless flow of love for self.

List your physical attributes that you believe are flaws:

_____   _____

_____   _____

_____   _____

_____   _____

_____   _____

Who told you these were flaws? _____

Why did you believe them? _____

_____

Song to Meditate On: "Flaws" by Kierra Sheard

Body
Treasuring Your Temple

When you've been physically abused, the last thing you want to do is love on your body. I know I did not want to do anything but hide my body. I tried everything to cover up from head to toe. If I could have walked around wrapped up like a mummy all day, I would have.

Some abuse victims turn to food, alcohol, drugs, sex, or even physical mutilation like cutting as a means to cope with the memories of the abuse. These vices, in turn, only cause damage (sometimes irreparable) to the body. 1 Corinthians 6:19-20 says, "Do you not know that your bodies are temples of the Holy Spirit, who is in you, whom you have received from God? You are not your own; you were bought at a price. Therefore honor God with your bodies."

Regardless of what we have suffered through, we should not put our bodies through even more pain by damaging it with any of the things I mentioned above. We are to treasure our temple, and that's what we will do once we move from abuse "victim" to abuse "survivor."

The article, My Body Is A Temple? 5 Ways To Treat The Human Body Right, offers great suggestions for how we are to treat our body:

1. Give it the Sabbath that it needs
2. Feed it with the right kinds of food
3. Eat the right amount of food
4. Give it exercise
5. Respect it as a body God made

Exercise: You Are What You Eat

In this exercise, you will build out your eating plan for the week. Include foods that promote Joy and Happiness.

Visit www.prevention.com for more information related to these foods and their amazing benefits:
- Walnuts and Flax - great in smoothies or in their raw form
- Pomegranate - lowers blood pressure, anxiety, and depression
- Yogurt and Kefir - enhances your populations of probiotic bacteria
- Dark Chocolate - loaded with polyphenols that boost your mood
- Apricots - packed with Vitamin B6 and antioxidants, beta carotene, lutein (great for eye health) and zeaxanthin (higher levels are linked to higher moods).

You Are What You Eat
Weekly Meal Plan

"If you keep good food in your fridge, you will eat good food." - Errick McAdams

Sunday:	Monday:
Breakfast - Snack - Lunch - Snack - Dinner -	Breakfast - Snack - Lunch - Snack - Dinner -
Tuesday:	Wednesday:
Breakfast - Snack - Lunch - Snack - Dinner -	Breakfast - Snack - Lunch - Snack - Dinner -
Thursday:	Friday:
Breakfast - Snack - Lunch - Snack - Dinner -	Breakfast - Snack - Lunch - Snack - Dinner -
Saturday:	
Breakfast - Snack - Lunch - Snack - Dinner -	

Exercise: Your Body Needs You!

In this exercise, you will jump-start your new lifestyle plan. Starting today, carve out 30 minutes in your day to get cardio daily. Here are some quick ideas to get you going:
- Brisk walking - either wear wrist and ankle weights while briskly walking, or use water bottles as exercise weights.
- Running/Jogging - If you like to run or jog, then run or jog.
- Try some of the fitness videos on YouTube if you like to workout at home.

Your body is a temple unto God. Treat it well, and it will treat you well. Love it, and it will love you back. Remember: Self-love doesn't just start in the mind and stay there. It flows from the mind to the body. So, take care of your body. Love yourself enough to take care of this body. It's the only one you will get!

Song to Meditate On: "Just One Touch" by Kim Walker-Smith

Your Body Needs You

"Warning: Exercise has been known to cause health and happiness." - Anonymous

Outline your weekly exercise plan for each day. It's okay to switch it up, if you'd like. But creating a routine for each day allows you to get out of your rut, get off your butt, and work your stuff.

Monday I will:
_____

Tuesday I will:
_____

Wednesday I will:
_____

Thursday I will:
_____

Friday I will:
_____

Saturday I will:
_____

Body

Uncovering the Hidden Gem

How many times have you tried to hide the beauty that is inside you? So many of us who have lived through a traumatic experience will wear a mask to cover who we really are. We don't want anyone to see that we are still broken; we are still in recovery; we still drink every now and then, or whatever your "thing" might be. We are still working through our healing. I know that was once me.

I had one mask for my family, one for business, and one for the people I called friends. I wore so many masks I sometimes forgot which one I was supposed to be that day. **Celebrity Relationship and Family Therapist, Spirit**, talks about how we have different color masks we wear that will attract people who like that color mask (let's say it's red), and our needs are not being met because underneath the mask, we are really lilac. So, we end up in the wrong relationships with people who can't handle who we truly are, and we are constantly trying to measure up to who they thought we were. You can watch the full video here [The Psychology of Compatibility](#).

Can you imagine the toll this can take on your body? It's difficult playing different versions of yourself all day long. At some point, your body will feel it, and what will you do?

Exercise: Box it Out!

Boxing is such a great way to get your blood flowing. When your blood flows, it allows oxygen to flow to your brain. You begin to see things more clearly. You can envision yourself as the strong person you have always been. No more masks to hide who you are. With boxing, you can imagine your abuser as your opponent in the ring, and this time you WILL WIN the fight!

Box it Out!

"You never lose until you actually give up." - Mike Tyson

If you have boxing gloves, put them on.

If not, it's okay. Ball up your fists and let's get to work!

1. Either stand in front of your mirror or turn on a boxing fitness routine on YouTube to get you motivated
2. Close your eyes
3. Take three (3) deep breaths in through your nose and slowly out through your mouth
4. Envision your abuser(s) is in front of you, and you are in the boxing ring
5. You have on protective gear so as not to hurt that amazing face God gave you
6. Assume the boxer stance; one foot extended out in front of you, knees slightly bent on both sides, fists up either in front or to the sides of your face
7. Open your eyes so you can see in front of you
8. Now, BOX the mess out of your abuser and don't stop until he/she its the ground

Exercise: Unmask and Uncover

Now that you've discovered another side of you through boxing, it's time to uncover the hidden gem inside of you. You've worn the mask(s) long enough. It's time to unmask to uncover who God created you to be. Men, you are smart, handsome, strong, brave, full of hope, compassionate and wise. You carry the seed of life. Your love for self and others runs deep and wide. You carry the load well, and you don't break under pressure.

Ladies, you are intelligent, beautiful, unique, a designer's original. You hold the love of God in your heart. You are fun, desirable, understanding and powerful. You water the seed of life and bring it to fruition. You love from a whole and complete place within you with nothing lacking or

missing. You are not afraid to ask for help, and you bring wisdom and sound counsel to every interaction.

Unmask and Uncover

"We all wear masks, and the time comes when we cannot remove them without removing some of our own skin." - Andre Berthiaume

I got so burned out from wearing so many different masks. It was literally exhausting and putting a toll on me that I didn't even realize until I fully uncovered myself and allowed my true self to be exposed. What was I hiding? I mean, seriously, what was it about me that I wanted to hide from others? I was trying to hide what others had done to me. It was as if I wore their damaged souls like clothing on my body. I needed to strip it all away. I needed to unmask in order to uncover who I was, not who I became because of the abuse. Are you ready to unmask and lay down your weight?

The following exercise was found at THE MASKS WE WEAR Psychology 12 ACTIVITY: THE MASKS WE WEAR

- Create the various masks you wear each day. I wore anywhere from three to four different masks each day.
- One the **outside of the mask**, put the faces that you show your family, friends, co-workers, each day. Feel free to create the masks however you want to. You can use paint, drawings, magazine cut-outs, poems, whatever. Just create the various faces you show in society each day.
- On the **inside of the mask**, create who you really are. The inside of your mask could look completely opposite from the outside or it may have some similarities. You won't know until you create it.

WHAT'S NEXT?

Then, I want you to write a paragraph that explains the significance of the words, images, etc. you used to depict your masks.

_____

_____

_____

_____

_____

Now it's time to drop the mask in order to drop the weight that has held you in bondage.

Song to Meditate On: "Break the Shell" by India.Arie

MODULE THREE

SOUL

Soul

Soul Cleansing

Now we understand the impact of trauma on our mind and our body, but what about the soul? Our soul is what makes us a complete and whole human being. When the soul is tainted and impacted from the stain of our trauma, it needs to go through a deep cleaning process. Similar to how when our carpets get dirty from all of the walking we do back and forth, our souls have been walked on time and again from the initial traumatic experience to every time we think about it and relive it in our mind.

We fill ourselves with so much negativity. No wonder it is difficult to love ourselves. Enough is enough. If we can clean our house, our car, our clothes, our desk at work…we can clean our soul by getting rid of all the junk that's been lodged there, and truly live from a soul that has been cleared out.

So, how do we clean the soul? I'm glad you asked. In these exercises, you will begin the process to clean your soul so that the enemy has nothing left to attach himself to as it relates to your trauma.

SOUL
- Soul Cleansing
- Forgiveness
- The Power of Connections
- Gratefulness

Exercise: The Trash can

In this exercise, you will create a physical or mental trash can where you will throw away all negativity. Once you have determined everything negative that must go, then you will fill yourself up with the good things you desire.

The Trash can

"Everything that touches YOUR life must be an instrument of YOUR liberation and tossed into the trash cans of HISTORY." - John Henrik Clarke

Our lives are filled with so much negativity that it's hard to fill our soul up with joy and positivity. From the news to the people around us to the voices in our head, the negativity can impact us daily. We need an outlet; somewhere to let all of the trash go so that we can fill ourselves with Happiness, Joy, and Freedom.

In this exercise, I want you to think about how you can go from dumping all of your trash to being filled and renewed.

Above, you see a trash can and a cup. In the chart below, list the **10 negative things** you want to throw into the trash can. Then, list the **10 positive things** you want to fill your cup with.

Trash can	Cup

Now that you've made your lists, you can either cut out the chart into individual slips of paper that you will actually throw away in the trash can (the negative ones), and tape the positive ones all around your house, car, desk at work…anywhere you will see them.

Exercise: What's in Your Mouth?

Have you ever really listened to yourself; I mean really listened to the words coming out of your mouth? I used to say, "I'm so stupid." "I'll never be able to figure this out." Those toxic words were holding me back without me even realizing it. I was so quick to say those words because they were what was said to me all the time I was growing up.

When our minds have been conditioned to believe something about ourselves that is not true, the words find a home in our souls, and our mouths will quickly open up to share with anyone who will listen.

It's time to detoxify our mouth in order to cleanse our soul!

What's In Your Mouth?

"Words can inspire, and words can destroy. Choose yours well." - Robin Sharma

Our lives are filled with so much negativity that it's hard to fill our soul up with joy and positivity. From the news to the people around us to the voices in our head, the negativity can overtake us. We have to know when we've taken in too much of it. What fills you also fuels you, so if you are filled with negativity, that is what fuels your life.

If all we do is go on social media, listen to the radio or watch television, or sit in the house and mope around, we will not have anything positive to draw from. So, we have to create it for ourselves.

Earlier in the program, we did an exercise called, "I Love Me." In that exercise, you listed 12 reasons why you love yourself. They were written similar to affirmations. I want you to create more affirmations that you will speak over your life. Below is the big mouth emoji with lines next to it. On those lines, you will write new I AM affirmations using one word. For example: I AM Powerful.

Song to Meditate On: "Fill Me Up" by Tasha Cobb Leonard

Soul

The Power of Connections

There is something about having powerful, meaningful connections in your life that will literally propel you to higher heights than you could go without them. God designed us to be in relationship with other people, especially people that are wise and offer good counsel. His word says in Proverbs 13:20, "He that walketh with wise men shall be wise: but a companion of fools shall be destroyed."

In the process of loving yourself, you must surround yourself with the right people. My coach calls them your Divine Escorts. These are the people God places in your life to help you walk through any circumstance with power and authority. Your soul needs people like this. It doesn't matter if you are male or female, we all need Divine Escorts to be with us along our life's journey.

When you are connected to the right people, the right things begin to happen for you. At the time of creating this coaching program for you, I became a certified life coach. I wanted to invest in myself so that I could invest in you. I love myself enough to invest in myself and surround myself with the right people. The women I connected with in that program have now become escorts for me as I journey through this next phase of my life. Who are you surrounding yourself with on your self-love journey?

Exercise: My Divine Escorts

In this exercise, you will identify those people who have either already walked the path you are walking, and they are now thriving, or they can be people who are with you side-by-side helping to hold you up like Aaron and Hur did for Moses in the Bible. Who are your divine escorts?

My Divine Escorts

"I want people in my life who are more interested in my growth than my comfort."
- Eric Johnson

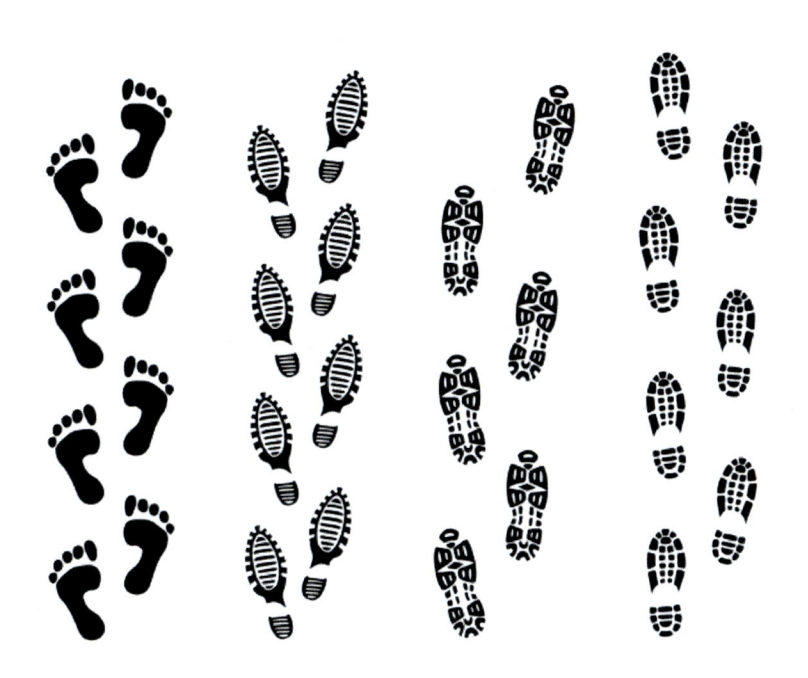

Divine Escorts have either walked your walk, or they will walk beside you to help you through your self-love journey. They leave footprints you can follow so you don't feel like you have to figure it all out on your own. Who has the Lord placed in your life to walk with you on this journey?

Who has walked your path?

List the people who have been on the same or a similar journey as you, and they have been there to help you understand how to walk through your journey with grace. Also, list how they have supported you; what specifically have they done?

My Escorts	How did they support me?

Better Together

"Sometimes our light goes out, but is blown again into instant flame by an encounter with another human being." - Albert Schweitzer

God designed relationships. He knows we are better together, stronger together than apart. In the YouVersion Bible app devotional, Right People, Right Place, Right Plan, the author, Jentezen Franklin, says:

"The people you surround yourself with determine the person you will become. When you start bringing the right voices into your life, you'll begin to make the right choices as well. And once you start making the right choices, you get the right connections. Every time God does something significant in our lives, He introduces us to new people—ones who are connected to our destiny and purpose. Learning to discern God's voice and follow His leading will remove you from bad relationships and bring you into contact with the right people.

Character discernment helps you avoid toxic entanglements. What is character discernment? It's the ability to recognize and embrace relationships that are good for you and to recognize and avoid those that are not. If you have a history of toxic relationships, you may need to develop this skill."

Franklin goes on to talk about "Flesh People vs. Faith People." Flesh people tear you down and make you feel unworthy. Sounds like our abusers, right? Faith people build you up, encourage you to fulfill the purpose God placed you here for. We all need Faith People in our lives.

Exercise: Thanks to My Faith People

In this exercise, thinking back to your Divine Escorts and what they have done to guide your self-love path and build you up when you were on your last leg, write them a letter of thanks. Tell them how much you appreciate them. If you feel inclined, you can share the letter with them when you feel ready.

Song to Meditate On: "Count on Me" by Whitney Houston and CeCe Winans

Thanks to My Faith People

"We must find time to stop and thank the people who make a difference in our lives." - John F. Kennedy

You can use these pages to write letters to your top three (3) faith people, or you can use your notebook/journal.

Thank you, _____, for _____

_____

_____

_____

_____

_____

_____

_____

_____

_____

_____

Thanks to My Faith People

"We must find time to stop and thank the people who make a difference in our lives." - John F. Kennedy

Thank you, _____, for _____

_____

_____

_____

_____

_____

_____

_____

_____

_____

_____

_____

Thanks to My Faith People

"We must find time to stop and thank the people who make a difference in our lives." - John F. Kennedy

Thank you, _____, for _____

_____

_____

_____

_____

_____

_____

_____

_____

_____

_____

Soul

Forgiveness

Forgiveness essentially saved my life. When I was able to forgive those who abused me, I became free to live the life God intended for me to live. That's what He wants for you, too. Forgiveness is not for the other person. It is for you, so that you can live whole again.

God wants for us to forgive so badly that He says in Ephesians 4: 32, "Be kind and compassionate to one another, forgiving one another, just as in Christ God forgave you." You may be thinking, "How can I ever forgive him for what he did to me?" Trust me, I thought the same thing. In no way am I saying forgiveness is easy or quick. There are layers to the forgiveness thing. When you decide to truly forgive, you have to walk in it, breathe it and operate from a place of love in your heart. Forgiveness does not mean you have to be friends with the person. It doesn't mean they get an open invitation to your current life. It just means you wish them no harm, you are cordial if in their presence, and you move along with your life.

Let's work on forgiveness!

Exercise: Whose Approval are You Seeking?

Forgiveness can be tied to other people who are connected to the person you need to forgive. You may have been abused by a family member, like I was. Then you feel like you can't forgive the person because other people in your family will be upset that either you told a family secret or because you are even thinking about forgiving the person. Let me tell you something, you don't need anyone's approval in order to forgive. God said we are to forgive, and that settles it.

Let's discover whose approval you are seeking so you can get over it and forgive.

Whose Approval are You Seeking?

"Instead of questioning why someone doesn't approve of your choices, ask yourself, 'Why do I need their approval in the first place?'" - Sonya Parker

You are approved to do anything you want to do in your own way, and in your own time. That's the great thing about forgiveness. You get to decide when you are ready to forgive those who have hurt you. You also get to decide when you will forgive yourself for carrying the burden of your trauma for all these years.

Some of my family members were angry with me for exposing my abuser. So, when it came time for me to forgive him, it was like I was committing a cardinal sin. But, the sin was actually me not forgiving him all those years. I had to make the decision that I did not care what anyone thought or said about me when I chose to forgive him. Remember, I was forgiving him so I could be set free from the pain he caused me. What he chose to do with my forgiveness was up to him.

Who is it that you feel won't let you forgive those who hurt you? List them below, and explain why you've been waiting for their approval to move forward with your healing process. Use your notebook/journal if you need extra space to write.

1. _____

   _____

   _____

2. _____

   _____

   _____

3. _____

   _____

   _____

Now that you've identified them and explained why you've been waiting for their approval, are you ready to move forward with forgiving those who abused and traumatized you whether others approve or not?

Yes _____   No _____

If you said no, schedule a one-on-one with me so we can discuss.

Exercise: I Forgive Myself

It's one thing to forgive the person who brought you harm. It's another thing to forgive yourself for holding on to your pain. One of the greatest things about self-love is that it is available to you anytime you are ready for it. Once you let go of your pain, you become open to the love you've always needed – Your Own!

In this exercise, you will write a letter of forgiveness to yourself for carrying your trauma like a child carries his backpack to school. You've packed all your hurt, pain, anger, frustration, bitterness, resentment, and shame in that backpack, and you've carried it around with you for years hoping someone else would remove the bag from your back. It's time you do it all on your own.

Song to Meditate On: "Forgiveness" by TobyMac ft. Lecrae

I Forgive Myself

"Offer yourself the same forgiveness that you've shared with others. You are deserving."
- Alex Elle

This will be one of the most challenging exercises of this program. Forgiving myself, and recognizing that what was done to me was not my fault, was one of my hardest things I ever had to do. But it had to be done, and now you must do it too. Be willing to forgive yourself so you can set your wings free to fly in every area of your life.

I AM WILLING TO FORGIVE MYSELF

I am willing to forgive myself because _____

_____

_____

_____

_____

_____

_____

_____

_____

Soul

Gratitude

Can you believe it? We are now coming to the end of our Just As I Am: 12 Steps to Self-Love journey. I am so grateful you stayed the course and did not give up on yourself. You are more than deserving to have the kind of love you deserve, and that love is already deep inside of you.

Your soul has been through so much. This whole process has been like putting your soul through the wash cycle, and now that you're in the drying off cycle, your continued work begins.

It's time you celebrate your wins. What are you grateful for as a part of this 12-week program? What did you discover about yourself?

Exercise: Celebrating My Wins

You've done such great work. Oftentimes, when we've been abused it is difficult for us to celebrate ourselves. But now, we are on the other side. We don't care about our abusers any longer because we love ourselves enough to let it all go. We are free, and we are freeing them as well. They don't deserve to take up any space in our souls any longer. It's time to celebrate your wins.

Celebrating My Wins

"This is the day which the LORD hath made; we will rejoice and be glad in it." - Psalms 118:24

What did you discover about yourself during these 12 weeks, the things you never realized about yourself before?

_____

_____

_____

_____

_____

_____

_____

How will you celebrate all that you've overcome?

_____

_____

_____

_____

Copyright © 2021 Haughton's Love LLC

Just As I Am: 12 Steps to Self-Love Coaching Workbook

Soul

Gratitude

des·ti·ny

/ˈdestinē/
noun

1. the events that will necessarily happen to a particular person or thing in the future.

Your destiny is yours. No matter what others have done to you, your destiny will come to pass. You have to see it in your mind and believe it in your heart so that your destiny can begin to manifest in your life.

The brokenness that you once felt was holding you back. Your whole and healed soul can now reach it's destiny. You've traveled the long path to get here, but when you look back at your life and look forward to what is ahead, you will see that everything you have been through was worth it. You are filled with love.

Exercise: Steps to My Destiny

Now that you've celebrated your wins, envision the destiny that God has for you. It's big. It's beautiful. It's more than you will ever imagine. What do you see along the steps to your destiny? It's time to climb them and see what you find.

Song to Meditate On: *"Loved by You" by Travis Greene*

Steps to My Destiny

"There are no wrong turnings. Only paths we had not known, we were meant to walk." - Guy Gavriel Kay

Take some time to envision where you see yourself in the next 5, 10, 20 years. Your destiny awaits you. As you begin to imagine the destiny that awaits, think even bigger than what you are thinking now.

- Close your eyes
- Imagine the life God has for you
- Envision yourself walking up each step
- What's on each step?
    - Do you see joy, hope, love?
- You must be smiling by now. I'm smiling for you.

On each step of the staircase to your destiny below, write the words/things that come to your mind as a part of your visioning exercise.

I'M GRATEFUL!

You made it like I knew you would. The **Just As I Am: 12 Steps to Self-Love Program** was designed to help you understand that God loves you just as you are. All throughout our time together, my hope was that you would learn to love yourself just as you are. You are enough!

I am so very proud of you for digging up all your old soul wounds in order to get to a place of loving yourself from a whole and complete place. I know it wasn't easy. I promise you, I know! But now that you are at the end of the program, it's time you begin to think about **What's Next**!

I have two final exercises before you go:

1. Grab a post-it note and write in big letters, "JUST AS I AM!" No one else needs to know what that means but you.
2. The last few pages of this workbook is your Gratitude Journal. For the next seven (7) days, write out the things you are grateful for about yourself, your life, work, family, friends. Whatever it is, just write about it and reflect on how great God has been to you.

I appreciate you for believing in me as your coach and believing that you were worth it all along. For more ways to work with me, visit www.BTSHTP.org.

Sincerely,

Latarsha Haughton

Your Self-Love Coach

GRATITUDE JOURNAL

_____

_____

_____

_____

_____

_____

_____

_____

_____

_____

_____

_____

_____

_____

GRATITUDE JOURNAL

GRATITUDE JOURNAL

GRATITUDE JOURNAL

GRATITUDE JOURNAL

GRATITUDE JOURNAL

GRATITUDE JOURNAL

Resources

There are a number of books that helped me along my journey to self-love. These books either focus on the Mind, the Body, or the Soul - all of the areas we worked through during our time together. I would encourage you to add some of these books as resources in your self-love arsenal.

Books related to the Mind:
- *The Battlefield of the Mind* by Joyce Meyer
- *Emotionally Destructive Relationships* by Leslie Vernick

Books related to the Body:
- *The Healing Secret of the Ages* by Catherine Ponder
- *Feelings Buried Alive Never Die* by Karol Truman

Books related to the Soul:
- *The Road Back to You* by Ian Morgan Cron and Suzanne Stabile
- *Breaking Toxic Soul Ties* by Tom Brown

Made in the USA
Columbia, SC
08 August 2023